# A DEEP ABSTRACTION

# DANIEL JOHNSON

Published by Glass Spider Publishing
www.glassspiderpublishing.com
Copy Editor and Typesetter Vince Font
Cover art by Morgan Thomas
www.morganthomasmusic.com/art-gallery
Cover design by Judith S. Design & Creativity
www.judithsdesign.com

GLASSSPIDERPUBLISHING

This is a book about many things—truth, survival, bravery, things we all go through. It's about struggle and overcoming adversity.

*This book is dedicated to my family.*

# CONTENTS

# CHAPTER 1

Demons to cleanse
Precise movements
My core amplified
No disguise
My convoluted ways
Days of grey
A place I will not stay
If you look close enough you will see
Confront adversity

What I have built over time
Seeing some kind of a sign
The great beyond
That morbid, sordid world is gone
Ascending within
Pushing onward

This power coursing through my veins
What I went through to get here

My tactics evolve
Problems I have solved
A lucid place
Somewhere full of grace
When I get lost, I always find my way home
Over the years, how I have grown
A liminal experience
Train of thought

Everything went dark
And all hope vanished
I screamed and no one heard
I opened my eyes
I raised my fist, I climbed
My aching heart was open
I transformed into something necessary
I knew what it was like to be free

What I convey to others
What I put together
What I discover
Such a passion for this life
A different type

A longing to be filled
An enemy to kill
When things are calm and still
Seeking refuge
Ending self-abuse

A desperate cry for help
Help yourself
Sinking deeper into an abyss
I will not fade away
I purified the decay
Embrace the dark
Reaching so far
Nothing can take away who you are

I will not be a slave
Dispose of all the pain
Cast out the negativity
Be grateful to be alive
Feel the vibe
Wisdom and insight
It shines so bright

Our lives will live forever
Feeling so much better
This constant endeavor

Hanging on to life
The weight on my shoulders gets lighter
Feeling visceral
I am on another plane
What I have framed
Need to maintain

The madness subsides
Clarity awakens
Facing yourself
So far above
Something within guiding you
This entity living inside you

Open your mind
This life is such a mystery
Courage, bravery
Searching for inspiration
Intense determination
What this journey has taught me
Finding the key to salvation
A new direction
With the strength of stone

What lies in the vast space of the psyche
I have been redeemed

I had to fight so fucking hard
It's so worth it in the end
Everything I will defend
You can find meaning and purpose
It's never worthless
Being reborn

I made it to the other side
I will never look back
Everything I am made of
Everything I lack
Those of us who are unseen
An approach so keen
What happens when you believe
A place so serene

These mechanisms working, functioning
Something beyond words
Despair I am escaping
Carrying myself through this
These transparencies in the shadows
This tranquil impassivity
Liberate the oppression

When my illness gets in the way
Torn apart from the inside

Feeling so trapped
I must break out of this mortal shell
Break these binds
In the midst of the night
I will make things right
Searching for the truth

Self-realization
Consecrated to my survival, and importance
The trust I lost
Must forgive yourself
Must clear your mind
A strong asset

The hardest kind
What we all come to find
Keep your head up
Capture a moment of beauty
It's been so long fixing what went wrong
I was spiraling out of control
I reached out for something
But it all just slipped away
It took time, but I found deliverance

This relentless battle
This cunning vision

Attached to something pure
The path I chose
What I have conceived
This life I will consume

A humane nature
Intuition towards another
The most high mentality
Individuality
Learn to shape your reality
This war raging inside me
Always have my honor
Create harmony out of chaos
A rapture appeared
Everything was clear

Dwelling in absence
Must let go
Annihilate my foes
Face the damage
Something lurking deep within
It was so hard to kill

Growing tired of waiting
Needing a change
Believe you will win

I have failed myself
I have saved myself

Follow my instinct
My spirit invigorated
Breaking down barriers
Things worth fighting for
A push in the right direction

Be inventive
Lift yourself up
I will get what I deserve
I have given all that I can give
This requisite taking me to new lands
Things moving into place
Never thought I would make it this far
This life can be so tragic
Also so blissful

So much inner gravity
This presence within
A curse turned into a gift
Rescue myself from this devastation

It can be so difficult
What I am up against
Believe in who you are
Solving a mystery
When you are living without
I have swam across oceans
I have had my doubts
Living spiritually
Everything that I condemn
Searching for an end

Walls closing in on me
My mind playing tricks on me
Mind displacement
Experimentation with the process
Never any fallacies

Finding where I belong
Trying so hard to fix myself
I just want my freedom
What I let pass me by
Ascend into the skies
Finding Zen

Not always a bad thing to be different
I won't be the victim anymore

No longer broken and sore
It took some work to change
Cleaning the stain
Moving on with life
So much ahead

I will live to fight another day
Absorbing sun rays
A place that ripped my heart out
This life so intriguing
Such powerful beings
Find your own answers
Something the mind creates

Those who have not been through what I have
Full of ambition and drive
Looking beyond
It's been such a long journey
This universe deep inside
There is time to make things right
Victory will be mine
Give yourself a reason to live

Something bigger than myself
Violence and peace
When my symptoms increase

I will not let this win
Everywhere I have been

As the sun and moon rise and set
Letting go of all regret
This hope never deteriorated
There is no forgiveness
When it passes and the good returns

Absorbing the light
Such revealing heights
I was trapped beneath, I rose
A way through was exposed
An amazing experience
Nothing can stop me now
Don't bring yourself down

Everything I need is in me
A head full of bad memories
This vessel holding my spirit
Pushing myself to new horizons
Something echoing beyond
Learning to let go
This world I transcend
Capture every moment until my end
Seeing things no one has seen

These concepts are forming
These notions are soaring
All my imperfections
Go your own direction
What some of us go through
A darker side
The mind's eye
There is a sickness in me
Being aware of your inner self
When I could use a little help

Things I need to change
When I'm worried about my life
When you need to save yourself
Pulling out a jagged knife
Does he not care?
Into a void I stared
What I will truly seek

Keep looking forward
What I have lived through
Made me what I am
Maybe you're already there you just need to see it
Feel it believe it
Something eternal it fills you
My mind is awake

What I will not forsake
When you need something on your side

Something pulling me back
Holding me back
I will take back everything he took away
I lost so many years
My spirit torn and frayed

Something worth having
It's up to me
Just keep breathing
Feeling so trapped
Trying to get out
A profound healing
Still alive
I learned that I was more
We create ourselves
We open that door

Never give in
No longer so wretched
The worst of it has ended
Greatness comes from defiance
I was so lost searching for truth
The way out is through

Exploring existence
Something in the distance
It is up to you to end the suffering

A world so bleak yet so meaningful
I will not sever my connection
Deep reflection
When it feels like I am fading away
The mind so powerful
My soul and the sky combine
So much stability
Discover solace
The feel of sunlight after being locked in a
dungeon
Less vulnerability
Empowering vitality
It's never too late
Something to relieve the pressure
So medicated so vindicated

There was this aftermath
I slowly got past
Somewhere free at last
Those of us who know the darkness
Reaching a breaking point
This structure so secure

The way you see yourself
Something leading me somewhere
Who you choose to be


Breathe it in
Take it in
Let it take you places that you've never been
Let it bring you hope
Let it bring you closer, it's never over
Nothing and no one will take away who I am
A crack in the ice coming towards you
Icy waters below
In the darkest night it glows
The killing and the suffering
When god's not really there
Always believed in the soul
Survive the bad parts to see the good
Making things the way it should be
It will grow
In the light within


A new direction
Clean the infection
When my issues get in the way
Working toward stability

After the fall
What you do to get back

What you use to extract the cancer
Everything you refuse
Something ripping me away
Pulling me down
Don't let it get to you
Let it take you away
A place you're trying to stay
Become alive, let the truth be your guide
We are so powerful
What was empty is now full
What was numb is running through me

Those I can connect with make it easier
Figure out what all this is for
Unleash your core, taken by force
Something clouding my vision
Learning to control my mind
My abilities, what I reconstructed

When the universe is against you
So many issues
A realization appears
Seeing for the first time

Just let me live my life
I need to believe
There is more than just suffering
Something I need to get out of me

When my head is tranquil
Trying to be grateful
Learn to appreciate what you have
You will find more
What this journey has taught me
The demons that have haunted me
When life takes a lot
I get caught
I get stuck
I pick myself back up
So much that disrupts
Fixing myself it takes time
Just living in this moment
Whatever may come
Whatever it takes

Beginning to see how important this is
Don't take it for granted
I was so abandoned
Some kind of illusion
When you stop letting it bring you down

What we have found
I believe that I will face this, I will win
Protect what's worth protecting
When it fills you up
Always looking for more
A path to righteousness
Focus on the good
Whatever makes it easier
Caring, not caring
My mind keeps staring

The more things change
Wherever we may go
A positive flow
As time flows
That eye inside showing you the right direction
Everything I have learned

Always ready for a battle
Ready for whatever comes
A subjective state
Never susceptible
It's never too late
Everything we destroy
Everything we create

The blood that's flowing
The air you're breathing
My mind playing tricks on me
Believe in your higher self
A curse that is fading
Know yourself

I can see the change in me
Everything I need is in me
A healing of impurities
Something always in the way
Taking control of it
Nothing can stop me

I have found a better place
A dark side that I embrace
I was put on this earth for a reason
The chemicals inside my brain
I know that I am sane
This demon I hate
I will evacuate
The days it shines brighter
When the weight feels lighter
Coping with this reality
Make the most of it while you're here
Be sincere

Something bad in you
Born with issues
Went through so much to get here
So much damage to fix
Use all of my strength to break free

When I wish it would all go away
When it gets worse
Hope for better days
So much perseverance
So much patience
What it takes to survive
The way you look at it
Look inside
Open your mind's eye
This path I walk never alone

There are forces at work
Can you see them?
Something against me
Something with me
I will overpower it
The above, the below
An awakening

This echo inside my head
A constant cycle
Don't feed the monster
Won't let my troubles get the best of me
The dimensions I have travelled
There is time to put it back together
These moments all combined
Dismantle what I am fighting
A gaze with directness
Uncovering what remains
Building a balanced system
Here I am this conscious being
This organic motion
Step through
Feel it move through you
An intense experience
Deep within
So vigorous
Staying vigilant

My world I have created
What I have destroyed
What I have evaded
There was a consequential action
Something strong that spread
An abolishment, an end

End the nightmare
Push forward with everything I have
A full heart
Moments of enjoyment

When I feel lost
I must believe
A divergent path
A powerful siege
Something high above pours into me
Feels so serene
Nourishing the soul
I have felt such cold
Out of the depths I climbed
I got left behind

What I make sense of
What I put together
My actions, my reactions
So deep this abstraction

Take control of this intrusive schizophrenic
experience
A strong will, a strong skill
It was all uphill
Just let go

I won't let it take control
My spirit it grows
Know your own truth
Never surrender what is mine

What we have all experienced
Feel the radiance
Knowing there's nothing wrong with you
Knowing there's more to you
Ascent into
Pushing onward
Desperate times, desperate measures
My life is on the line
What brings my life meaning
Explore a great beyond

A gift, a curse
When it's at its worst
All of my intentions
Fight the tension
Believe you are able
A world so fatal
A realm of beauty
A poison seeps into you
Just keep growing
Breathing, reaching, learning

A surge of life
The dawn after the night
Obtaining a keen insight

Out of the chaos came an oasis
I need to face this
So much grit
Don't take it for granted
Reinforce my world
I was left stranded
Pulled out by the current into the deep
Oscillating cycles

What your life depends on
Myself I rely on
Great patience
A higher power
A glimmer of hope that got brighter
A critical decisive point in time
A battle worth fighting
Everything I have seen

A ferocious push forward
The ability to see truth
My thoughts all connected
My soul resurrected

No more self-destruction
A supreme ambition
A deep incision

When life shines upon me
I absorb it, I take it in
It gives me strength
I will heal my wounds
Strive to be consistent
Such a powerful resistance
Persistence
I will tear it open to look inside

When there's nothing I can do
So high above I flew
My center intact
Movements towards something better, greater
Made it so far
So many scars
I pull out the nails so deep
Everything you seek

Something reaching out to me
Something helping me
Stay positive
Whatever it takes

So much at stake
Everything left in my wake
My technique is great
On my shoulders this weight

Difficult times
These movements within
A crusade of great purpose
As I travel further
Finding something unknown
The truth I convey
The illusions going through my mind
Threatening distortions
When life wears away at me
All you can do is survive
Stressed out of my mind

I will not be the victim
A march to victory
The tragedy that took hold
Face the cold
Pushed over the edge
Against so much
The inner nature
A hard reality to embrace
Never had it easy

Still breathing
An optimistic approach
Control of the mind
Was there a fate I could not escape
Look to the future

A signal sent to me that I never got
Do I have what it takes
What it is that I need
What kept me going
When it's not enough
Using a process
A philosophy

Adversity was my adversary
So much bravery
When life is attacking me
A part of me that's different

When it's so revolting
Wake up rise against
What I will destroy
What I will cure
Peace and Zen will break through
Take back, discover
What is yours

How I was made
What I am made of

Barely made it out alive
Wisdom arrives
Here I thrive
There is more to be
A better side
Where there is content
What I give form to
There's only so much I can take
Something grim keeping me going
Pushing me against an army
Do whatever it takes

At full capacity
Erase the tragedy
So much stability
A victory inevitable
Letting go of everything
Places you can reach
It's endless
The reason we are here

# CHAPTER 2

I have always known there's more
Everything in store
Opening these doors
Where the truth lies
Looking to the skies
So liberated
So invigorated
Let it pass
Let it die
When I don't know why
What we figure out along the way
Molded like clay

Overcome my adversity
When it feels like it's worth it
Self-worth
Self-respect

Searching for connection
A reason to live
Something to give
What put out will come back ten-fold
What the future holds
Come in out of the cold

I work so hard at this life
You have come so far
A light that slowly grows
Into something different
Closing in on it
Growing closer
Feeling so consoled
The times I am at ease
The life within is winning

What I was searching for, for so long
Appeared in front of me
Took away all my fear
Break through the silence
The times I feel so vibrant
What affects our lives
The spark that ignites into a flame

What I will always take with me
A feeling of security
What we are seeking
Getting better all of the time
What I can sense in others
What I can sense in myself

I was an outsider
Disconnected, suicidal, torn apart
There are others like me
Others who have broken free
So much happening deep inside
Calm like still waters

Taking in every moment
The scars deep inside
When it hurts
When I am just getting by
Finding comfort and congruency
In all the chaos
So much more ahead
So much life to feel
The light of the moon, it lives inside me

Get up off your knees
You must believe

The degree of force
My life I will redeem
What I have been chasing
This burden I'm erasing
There comes a point where you need to change

Something so elaborate
To form disillusion
This construct surpassing
The danger I am elapsing
The poison I'm extracting
Looking on in amazement
Never take it for granted
You only live once
How it happens you decide
I have fallen so many times
A metaphysical world opens up
Free to explore
Trying to earn it

I have done all that I can do
I grow tired from the battle
Music helps my condition
I will win my freedom
I travel through space and time
I will not be a slave to this

These powers of the mind
An acute position, this condition

Overwhelming discordance
Trying so hard to believe
So much conflict
Expel my inner demons
As we live throughout the seasons
When the beauty speaks to me
The hurt seeps into me
I know I will end it

There is something beyond
So medicated
The view so impressive
I will not live a derogatory existence
A heart full of hope
The aspects of this life, so compelling
The havoc we live through
Out of the death came life
A place you never want to see
Overtaken by the storm
I find myself so wounded and torn
Whatever keeps you alive
Something there for me to hold onto

This creation so tragic, so flawed
Yet I have felt so in awe
Figuring out why I am here
Flew so high above
Dragged so far below
Intense feelings
Slowly healing
The blinding light
Unique sight

Something to help you see
That door I locked, threw away the key
Every time I fall
Taking control, shaping it
There is hope for me
I'll never stop
Take a stand, understand
Kill it before it kills you
Caught trapped in time
Find your way out
Need to get out
Give it all you have
Stability throughout the chaos
Been through so much worse

There are ways through everything
I will find it
When I am so deep in it
What you discover
Strong upward battle
Importance used
Something deeply infused
A warrior against an army
Against the odds
Everything I depend on
The chance we have to learn and live
To walk this earth
Waking up from a bad dream
The way it all seems
A new level
A different plane
Say goodbye to all the pain
A steady course through violent waters
To induce life
What you get out of it
It is no longer threatening
Strong resolve
Can't keep looking down
All that you can miss
To emerge from nothingness
Into something together, whole

Sometimes it takes time, patience
The places you can reach
A world inside so beyond
It's all psychological
It opens, you step through
A prerequisite for growth
These algorithms
Making sense of it all
You can't run from your problems
Learn to appreciate what you have
Destroy the enemy

Feeling this elation
My creation
Stop the invasion
Can't comprehend the reason why
Watch it slowly fade and die
I have always known there is more
To be proud of what you have done
Absorbing the sun
I am not the only one
Push yourself
Popping pills just to maintain
Enveloped by shadows, frightening echoes

What happens beneath
My story is evolving
These calculations helping me determine
A great metamorphosis
Found the other side
I can feel the change moving through me
Why we are here
We all have our purpose
Disturbance in my function
Lost faith for a long time
Don't get caught in the hate
Move on to the next plane
Don't mind the rain
What you have lost, what you have gained
Control your focus
Hold on to this
Everything you fight with

A mode helping me discover
Let things be
Clear my mind
As you grow stronger
Something you find
When this life is not so kind
What we have overcome to get here

So high above I climbed
Take it all in
Whatever takes you there
To a place that heals
Dark clouds inside
Something to rise from
A strong heart
I had to face my past
It feels like I'm winning
With my reality I clash
Putting it all together
A will that never recedes
Our lives will live forever
What exists deep within

It flows into my spirit
Finding a secret
Must believe in this
Something out there
All that we have created
All that we have destroyed
What we must take back
All that I have conquered
A universe far within
Hold on to what you need
I fortify what I have built

A feeling of utopia
Everything opens up

There is so much courage among us
Wanderers discovering
Crush the opposition
Ascension
A weapon against it
Coming back to life all of the time
I refuse to give up
Will this take me where I need to go

I am beckoned to another land
If you believe you can
Everything I understand
Need to fail before you succeed
Have patience
You will find what you need
I fell away from everything
A little belief goes a long way

When it's so intense
A cerebral conception
It gets so complicated
My head is faded
Like the flow of a river

Constantly moving in a certain direction
Clean the infection
Searching for some kind of solace, relief
So amazing how far I have come
Holding on, letting go
What this life offers
Made my way through the labyrinth
My mind was so sick
Everything I have fixed

So intoxicated, so sedated
Make your own way
As the emptiness fades
I will not beg for my life anymore
He was never there when I needed him
A source inside
Leading me somewhere
Learning to care
There was a glimpse of beauty
That grew into a gaze
What's happening behind my eyes
Lonely cries from the depths
A frightful occurrence

Something reaching out to me
It's such a mystery

The beyond, such a journey
What I have was compelled
Bound to this spirit
A quest for absoluteness

I didn't come this far to fade away
I saved myself from myself
I got away
Those of us who are not the same
The past left a stain
Everything I became

A subjective process
Finding a connection
What you love is important
It transcends
Make the most of this life
What resides in the heart
There was an exponential growth
Further than the stars

How powerful the right mindset can be
Feeling so displaced
I will guide myself
When it feels like I am on my own
Something I have always possessed

Throughout all the wretch
Something you always take with you
So much more than just pain

Everything we've accomplished
Everything so corrupt
Form ideas
There are ways to cope
I will never conform
Surviving the storm
What your eye captures
The beauty all around us
Taking steps to better my life
What seemed so endless came to an end
Good things are happening, I can feel it
A growing wisdom
Trying to make some sense of it all
Some kind of cathexis
Look past the dismal tragedy
Catastrophe
This internal struggle continues
So many issues

Went through treatment to get well
In the end I rescued myself
From all the danger

I was a stranger
This path I have walked
I saw a light at the end
Those who are blessed, those who are not

All the chaos slowly disappears
A tranquil moment envelopes
Everything I have dissipated
All of my actions
I will not surrender my freedom
I will not be a slave to this sickness

Faith is a powerful thing
It does not have to be in god
No matter what I live through
My soul always intact
Continuously evolving as the years pass
So many mysterious things I've experienced

What I am composed of
What I am born of
A curse, a gift, a wish
Closer to bliss
A cool fall breeze
Breathe it in
From a disaster

Into a new world

This intriguing feeling
Keeps me moving
Keeps me finding
There are no delusions here
Overcome misfortune
I will take hold of it
A strong grasp
Everything that makes us alive
A methodical nature
What is beneath me now
These strong inner shrouds
Something opens
What are you fighting for
No longer so broken and sore
A massacre of this enemy

The times when I am beyond harm
Wounds that have healed
So fucking determined
All of this intention
So focused on where I'm going
So many demons
Everything I have seen has made me who I am

Sometimes life deals you a bad hand
You make the most of it
Exploring these possibilities
The hatred I feel, don't let it control you
New wings take me higher
All of my triumphs
All of my loss
These ecstatic movements
Powerful eccentricity
Learning I am not alone
This energy that surrounds us
It's within us
Decisive patterns
My soul in harmony with my mind

I question why
I think for myself
A destructive waste trying to seep into you
When inspiration hits you
The times I feel blessed
So much chaos, so much meaning
I will not lose my way

I have suffered through injustice
Came out the other side
I saw illumination

So much tragedy among us
Will we rise above this
So much more above this
Something happening deep within
Unique defects
A prolific, inventive instinct

What continues to haunt me
What I continue to see
So many years buried
This intrinsic experience
The human condition
A surpassing vision

What I have devised
So definitive
Knowing who you are
It gets so hard
How I react from it
Learning to control it
Being aware of it
Free myself from these bindings
We all hurt sometimes
The souls of mankind

I have seen a perfect place
I have done something great
We are not alone
Feel it deep in my bones
It's never over
Just that much closer
Something reaching into me
Changing me
So much more than all of this

Everything that defines us
What reminds me there is life beyond death
Wake up from the nightmare
What we turn to
Always believe in you
The rhythm, the melody, the motion
So captivating
It takes you places
It affects your reality
What helps you along your way
What shows you new horizons
Serenity, something higher

Let the sadness and the darkness pass
And fade away until it's gone
When it's not easy to move on

Stay strong
Straight from the heart
A new world opens up
I have forced myself through it all
I have built myself piece by piece
Revolving within the mind
Within this being
It's been with me all this time
Just had to release it
When I decided to stay in this world
What events that transpired
Everything I became
I know why I'm here now
I know where I'm going

The sky opens
I rise through it
Leaving the misery behind
I transcend it
The stress attacks that kill me inside
I look to the future
Always finding motivation

When humanity destroys itself
When we save ourselves
So relentless

This illness always interfering
I will earn it
Never look into the past too long
Something wrong
Hope is never gone
Something so meaningful it hits you
Feelings that swell
We will escape the hell
Believe in your life

Taking it all in
Something true I give
My power is growing
I can feel it flowing through me
Something so exquisite
It fills me
So complicated, so intricate

These sudden reveries
Making enhancements
Taking control
Don't sink into the depths
Don't tumble down that hole
This life can be so dubious

Wherever this leads you
A place so appeasing
A place I'm leaving
It takes time, patience
Be what you are and more
There are no limits, no boundaries
Keep moving through it
It's in your blood
It's what you were born with
A spiritual level
Everything I will settle
Everything I will let go of
Everything I will hold on to
Everything I need is inside me

The light breaks through and shines upon you
Showing you there's so much more
Something happened, I changed
Experienced new things
It is what you make it
Replenish the spirit
My intentions are clear
On a mission against fear
The ones who know me
Have such a powerful influence on my life

A deep compulsion
Guided by this cognition
I will reach remission
What it is to be free
Shadows all around me
Taken hostage by my own mind

A punch in the mouth
A straight jacket
The pills that take the pain away
I tried to die
This is such a pivotal time in my life
My eye wide open
Self-medicated
Being invaded
Been places you can't possibly imagine
I was so dead inside, now so alive
Instinct taking over
It's not over
Can you see the beauty
Growing immunity
Take in the moment
I have reached into the great unknown
I won't let this force me down
What this life requires.

# CHAPTER 3

Balance disrupted, mental proportions
Neurotic distortions, contortions, absorptions
Bleeding heart, the endless search for more
Descent into oblivion
Replenish the core
Escaping my history
Keep fighting towards victory
The rhythm of the soul
Crawling out of this hole
All of the things I have seen
The empty, the warmth, the cold
The answers will come
Full of strife
Full of fight
A sense of deliverance
Grateful for your life
I have found a way

A little further everyday
Guided through this night
By this inner sight
Assimilate technique
A vision unique
When you learn you grow
When you grow you live
I had to conquer hell so I did
Awaken in a new day
The past lay dead and bleeding
Emotions seething
A sacred illumination
A fascination with survival
Serenity in waves, moon rays, new days
Escaping a deceiving haze
Destructive mind gaze

All the times I have fallen
All the times I have failed
Redemption found
Inner shrouds
This burden forcing you down
A passion for the fight
It shines so bright
Opening a new dimension
A beautiful ascension

Surfacing after years of inner violence
These illusions distorting truth
All of this abuse
Desensitized to fear
Fuck the voice I hear
Searching for truth, freedom, solace
Defending what I have created
Feeling so elated
Evolution of the mind
Give me a sign
A self-embrace
The old me I erased
From devoid to complete

No more suffering
It's time to start living
Inspired to save this life of mine
Fighting this inner gravity
Know thyself when there's nothing else
A dreadful experience
An obscure appearance
Take back what is mine
An indestructible design
Keep pushing through it
A new world appears, one that I created
Slowly opening

Awakening abilities
Blissful ways
So much damage over the years
All the battles through my fears
Starting to heal
Starting to feel
The meaning behind everything

The darkness pulls me in
The light is changing me
The power of positive thought
All the life I have sought
I know I will make it
I know I will face it
This powerful force drives me
Guides me
A source of life
Take a look inside
See what you will find
Feelings that haunt me
This dynamic movement
Augmented strength
Myself I thank

Attrition through my inner wars
I never felt like this before

When it rains it pours
My domain it soars
Become something more
Break through
Hard times we all go through
We all must unite
We all must fight
Escape the torment
An impulse to destroy demons
We are not alone
Find your way home

This psychological prowess
Determination
This soul so powerful
Reaching a higher level
Exploration, inner growth
A reflection of self
Finding something real
Hold on to it tightly
Master your reality and your fears
Coming back to life

Depravation
We are here to survive
I caught a glimpse through peaceful eyes

Waiting to see my dreams materialize
Climbing higher
Perpetual resolution, absolution
Chaos inside
A cataclysm of the mind
Radiant positive energy
Keeping me alive
It takes bravery
Searching for so long
Those moments where nothing can go wrong
Building a haven
Defeating solitude
My universe expanding
A new understanding
A secure hope

Finding solutions
Life is sometimes fragile
Is there some kind of salvation
Try to interpret this world
It's not all tragic
Something deadly inside me
When thoughts only make it worse
Push me to the edge
Isolated heart
Consuming addiction

Aching for the same
Release from within
Riveting horizons
I will win this battle
Recognizing patterns
Find awareness to enhance it
Diminished radiance
Strength is something you must create
Awake the light
Straining emotion
Perspectives of creation
Plentiful sensations
Overcoming tragedy
Trapped in this lunacy
A meaningful existence
Endless persistence
Left behind, intriguing signs, infested minds
Won't let myself waste away

Receptive to change
Suffering endured
Need something more
Searching for direction
Connection
Resurrection
Damaging relapse, collapse

Left to accept
The strength I have kept
Barriers accumulate in this distorted state
Take control
All the destruction
Never give up
As life fluctuates
New doors opening
Finding inner peace
Will this horror cease
Shivering in the coldness
Revealing metamorphosis
Captivating views

A spreading infection
Liberate myself from this broken and detached
place
This enemy I will destroy
My world was so severe
Reaching new heights
With fond surroundings
Things becoming clear
Work to keep control
To broaden my awareness
I will embrace as times change
Let myself heal

Looking for ways to cope
Keep your dreams alive
So unbearable
My encounters have dragged me down

Respect yourself
It takes time
Mind racing
Deal with the anger
Logic breaks it down
Utilize what I have learned
This place is what you make it
Your reality is what you make it
Infusing my understanding
Further and further, holding on
This is paralyzing, still surviving
Been too long being so far gone
Hold your head up high
Find a better way
Learn to live

Faith in self
Through sickness of soul
Lead me home
Regain power and control
Troubled densities

Embedded in me
Reaching out until I remember
Hope runs further in
Wounds will always mend
From hollowness
From nothingness
Aspirations fuel me
Left somewhere dark and alone
Pick myself back up again
Look within
The floods of thought
Negative extremes

Escape the descent
The weight on my spirit
So compelled to win
When there's something missing
Every reach, every shape
A higher self
Time heals, carried myself through the years
Find some balance
Made it through
Stayed true
Life is a trip
Have to be at one within when I slip

Hospitals, medication, the chemicals inside my
brain
The feelings that get too strong
My life that I sustain

Emerging from the depths
Uncovered my truth
Inner demons weakening
Fill the emptiness
The past mends
Buried beneath the surface
Where I was left faceless
Held on to what mattered most
A ghost longing to be free
The inside drifting further from the outside

Rise above with the deepest part of me
New planes of existence
When that door opens and the light is blinding
Getting closer
Isolation running through my veins
I tried to speak from that distant place
This reality eating away at me
All this world offers
So much to conquer
Find my own answers

Control the fear
It spreads like cancer
Reveal what I need to see
Extract a weapon
So transparent
Stronger frame of mind

Beautiful change
The views, the elevations
Climbing higher
Stared death in the face
This abyss of wonder
Why do we kill ourselves
Fixing broken spirit
Can't kill a strong soul
Won't let this take control
Beyond the madness
Creation, inspiration, dedication, desperation
Something separating me
The nightmares I have slayed
Face this pain
The dark makes the light gleam
The ways things seem
Wherever this may take me
Prove to yourself

This new energy
Evolving vivid states of mind

Mental illness
The good shit seems to fade
When I feel like a stranger here
When I lose control
Something holding me back
Deciphering my existence
Break through restraints
It adds to my strength
Levels of consciousness
How much can I take
See past the ruin
Into the deep
What I have learned
What I have found
My mind spins round
It seems I've gone every direction
I will rise, disconnected, wandering
Destruction, creation, all I've survived
Found a way deep inside
I have hit rock bottom
Fucked up so much
Over and over I get back up
Cluttered emotions

Dragged under, determined
Know when to let go
A dark presence
All the pain we induce
All the shit to refuse
All the days to win and lose

Once you cross that threshold
Into a better life
It comes together
A different sight
Could not make sense of it
Anger pulsating through me
Deluded by my own mind
Conquering elements
Repressed emotion
What does my future hold
My esoteric ways
Exhume this fortune
I devise, integrate
Sculpt the broken fragments
Parasites feeding on me slowly
When an opening appears
I persevered
The places I have reached

Against it all
Transformation

Endless battle
Fight to remain
I won't throw it away
Free to explore
A sick progression
Escape this infection of the mind
Fueled endeavors
We will survive
Seclusion, contorted being
Discover true wealth
Growing efficiency
Shit builds up
The world is corrupt
So much hate that disrupts

Exploring growth
Clearing my head
Use my abilities
Rediscovering what drives me
Determined to keep hope alive
Clouded element
Just want to get through it
When I feel like I'm frozen, broken

What I need to break free
Fighting a feeling that's tearing at my soul
What lies below
Sources of light
A higher level
A life force pours into me
Gazing into and through
It's not over for you yet
Deep within
The struggle for your life

Am I here for something more
Things need to change
That only I can change
I emerge from the death of my spirit
Fighting the sickness
Methods evolve
Things becoming clear
Look ahead with no boundaries
Every day is decisive
Bringing awareness into my function
Pondering solutions
Screaming inside trying to hide it
This world I defy it
The ideas that blossom

This out of place feeling
To the fullness of my being
Hard to move on from a place so far gone
Slowly healing
My abilities surpass my flaws
My truth is concrete
Filling the emptiness
Challenge boundaries
Beauty's sudden hand reaching out to us
Reinforce my surroundings
Push your limits
Can't stop me now
Rise above
Deeper than oceans
Elusive heights reached
Destruction of oppression
Eternal expression
Cultivating ideas
Solutions, answers
World forcing you down
Something hidden inside

Release from within
Signs of resilience
Face your mind
Putting shit together

Life severed
Lived in that world too long
Precision of thought
I fought and fought
Reaching new heights
Solace opening
Find a way to live
Endure the pain
Fight to be whole
Find a deeper level
This new hope running through me
Vitality restores
Hidden dimensions
Deciphering existence
Always learning
Not a slave anymore
Taking my life back
Deep inside it's been a ride
It opens wide it guides

Delirious movements
Spiral out of control
The spirit you will find
Take control of your mind
Reaching towards the sky
Does he hear our cries

Break down these walls around me
Severed attachment to this world
Try to accept
Reaching out reconnect
So much to rise above
So much to overcome
I will live free
I will die free
The search for inner peace
New energy running through me
Eradication of the past
Subdue this monster

Lurking in the shadows
Decrepit wandering
Immune to the waste
When this world spits in your face
Never lose your grace
You will find your place
It's not the destination it's the journey
Something to cure me
Something to assure me
Introvert a way out
Go beyond
Transcend reality
We all suffer

Heal yourself gradually
Reach out, keep each other alive
When everything was taken from me
I decided to fight
I found what was right

# CHAPTER 4

Realizing everything in front of me
Let it all be
Everything open, lucid, free
Whatever it takes
What's at stake
It's a long way down
My intrinsic movements
Surrounded by chaos
What belongs to you
Noticing clues
So much tragedy
We've accomplished so much
Will humanity survive itself

These constructive mechanisms
Leading me somewhere whole
Somewhere real

Don't let it control you
Something against me
Something also with me


I forced myself up
Slowly put it all together
What witnessing darkness does to you
What life has to offer
Search the beyond
Hope is never gone
When it's been too long
When there's something terribly wrong
Works its way into you
Must release
Wars for peace
Interaction with cerebral signals
A power leading you
Everything moving in circles
Through my mind
What is inhaled, what is exhaled
An intense surge pushing me, helping me live
We all have our battles, our wars
Deep in our core
What is all this for


How far our sight reaches

Show yourself, teach yourself
An exhilaration runs through me
An explosion of light
Feeding the soul
Everything is connected
Colorful horizons fading
Find an opening, with time and effort
An echoing of the beyond
The wind blows, skies of blue, the trees
Learn to appreciate it

So many unanswered questions
Where was this god back then when I needed him
Moving on with life
The deep night
I will remain
There is no disguise
This is what I am
Let it show through
Find the you in all of this
The path we choose
Make the most of this life

All we can do is live the best we can
Such efficiency
Helping me along my way

There was a divergence
Fighting lethargy
A disturbance
I fixed all the damage
Inner control
I was deep in lamentation
There was an immunity
What you put behind you
Everything that guides you

A worthy step in the right direction
Everything I reinforce
The calm after the storm
Fight to get back
Everything such a mess
It's never over
Following, exploring a paradigm
One day at a time
It all runs through me
Keep your head right
I could see it falling down all around me
The stress at a high degree
All I can do is suffer through
Wait for peace
It comes and it goes
Learn to live with it

Learn to let it go

It's always been there
Pulling me down, rise above it
I found virtue
Don't let it hurt you
Been so many places within
So many experiences
There's so much more to see
I will not be held back

Illation of what's real
Examining my within
What you choose to focus on can save your life
It can help you see
Whatever sets you free
What you choose to be
New meaning, new life, new reason

There is so much that goes through me
So much that grows in me
It's there if you can reach it
On this mission
A fucked up condition
All I have given
What it's like to feel human

To hit rock bottom
To make a difference
Redefine patterns
A path of entropy
Such intensity

Fight with emotion
Enhancing my capacity
Everything that's visible
It's all around us
This implement helps me to carry into effect
To fulfill, to accomplish
This interconnection
It's all working together
For my survival
Seeing further than I've ever seen
Reaching further than I've ever known
I have created this purge
To help me along my way
Putting things in perspective

Take away the apathy
There is so much to care about
Feel it all around you
Feel it in you
The music will give you strength

It is what you make it
Move past it
Giving life to anemia
The attributes we all have
Carrying us through
Choose to take a stand
It's up to you
The more you fight the better it gets

A higher level
Where this life takes us, in different directions
Ascending above it all
Where I was, that place will forever be gone
I have lived through great torment
Came out the other side still alive
Everything I possess
This potency taking affect
I was sucked into a void
What I survived created me

The atrocities of man
All the suffering we have caused
A banishment of pathogenesis
A prolific mind
How it feels to win
We will do it together

What we are will live forever
This consistency helping me stay whole
Something beyond words
Let go of the hate
Even if there is reason for it
It got too strong

A remarkable feat
What it is we seek
Break these bars
A prison of the mind
Learn to fly
It will take you where you have never been
Waking up from a nightmare
What we become
It's been such a struggle
The life inside, never let go of it
A way out of the shadows

It's in our nature to survive
So much adversity
There is so much beauty
Even if it's hard to see
Let it all pass
When it all slips away
A prospect of great importance

To reveal truth
Growing intensity
Deep in these reveries
Something in my head I don't know how it got
there
I will challenge it to the end
Reaching my own answers
When my instinct takes over
Illusions of fear
Cast them away
A place I have arrived
These demons interfering
Struggled through great calamity
Is this life a gift, or a curse
Self-worth
As a flower wilts
Everything I destroy
Everything I enjoy
Making sense of it all
What I am able to detect
There is time to make things right

When I find myself in need
With nothing to turn to
I learned self esteem
Everything positive I have seen

Powerful egression
Searching for direction
Led with apprehension
Into different experiences
This perpetual life continuously evolving

No one can take it away from me
I have earned everything I have
Everlasting transcendence
I was drowning in dangerous waters
So broken
As the years went by
I finally reached an end, also a beginning
A light shining in certain places
I will obtain what I have always needed
This substance keeping me alive
When I fall
When I have reached my breaking point
Patience, virtue

A strong magnanimous being
This freedom was invaded
The pain and suffering
What it means to be alive
I philosophize

Unexplainable things
As I grow everything opens up
My observation
The slowly fading devastation
I will repair what has been done
I will embrace all of this
The soul of the mind

No matter how bad it gets
Using my intellect
This is my catharsis
I reached a serious crisis
It changed me
Desperate times, desperate measures
Keep it together
Fucked up times, moving on

When you can't fix what you've done
I learned to live with it
What I became means something
A shift of motion
Ascending into a new world
Brain waves creating, functioning, using logic
A spiritual thing, a connection
When it all falls back on you
All the good moments

A struggle to realize
Some things take time
See it in yourself
No one can take that
These auditory hallucinations
I will prove wrong
Always working on this
A steady ongoing battle

Persistence of motion
I called to him, nothing was there
These wings to spread
It's so much better than it was
When you're deep into it
I will reach out indefinitely
Feeling different things
What this new faith in life will bring
I came so close to death
This life has much to offer
A fierce dedication
This comprehension

Everything I reckon
Using logic as a tool
Glad the worst is over
A passage into something great

A hunter of demons
No requiems
Focus on the life
I will not be overtaken by the nothingness
I will not desist
I will go on, pour your heart out

I will escape the peril
Be true to yourself
Never give up on yourself
What I built from the remnants
A spiritual experience
This life is such a mystery
Taking away the pain

An oracle whispered in my ear
A tendency to live on
I can feel the change run through me
I've got a disease
An original way
Against this hysteria
There is more you can realize
What I cast aside
The world can be so heartless
We will overcome it

My mind was sick, I had to recover
When it hits me like a train
When I am not the same
Doing what I can
What I will pursue into danger
I won't stop until my adversary is buried

Falling into illness, it eclipsed my lifeforce
Lost in need
Must repair myself
Purge my spirit
This candescence
Something bigger than myself
We all have our issues
We all feel pain
The forces at work
When you just want it to end
Elegies of the heart.

# CHAPTER 5

What you notice if you look hard enough
Discovery of one's self
We who escape hell
I made it out alive
Out of the cataclysm
Feel it growing from within

Everything we contain
Feeling sane
A feeling of loss
This longing for more
The life, the death
Felt so much wretch
I had to do something to change things

Still here creating this life
So much I devise

What you'll find, give it time
An intriguing design
What I can see in my mind
Slowly changing perspective
What I enter brings me closer
How much was taken
So hard I tried
A gradual change in my life
What my mania does to me

Tired of the struggle
The constant disruption
Finding answers
What logic tells me
A missing key
What we are up against
So fucking much I defy
When I just want it to be over
A heart as strong as stone
We are never alone
Use what you know
Devoted to my cause
I witnessed a miracle
We are born for a reason
The changing of the seasons

Concern for myself
My karma evolving
Feel the serenity
It helps to clear my mind
Developing gallantry
Fighting pathology
Be unique
Soaring out of the shadows
My bounds keep me balanced
These barriers won't stop me
Experience something good
Something you can get lost in
I will force it away
Purified
I buried the past
Focused on the now
How far I have come
Everything I have become
Release the dismay
Torn and frayed

A traveler of the soul
A quest for control
Very secure, stable, constructive
Embrace my defects
Threatening forces I must destroy

Everything I never deserved
Everything I have discovered
Just letting go
Lost in the sound
To that world no longer bound
So many times I have fallen
So many times I have ascended
I will initiate logic
I deserve what I have

My miscellaneous directions
I will not miscalculate
I will always be distinct
I am the weapon
I walk a difficult path
A transformation into something greater
What we are born into
What we have seen through
Had to wake up from this oppression
An existential portal
When I just want it to be over
When I am so grateful

We are all searching for answers
In this world of chaos, an unfolding harmony
Disabling neurosis and trauma, hard to get past

When it feels good to be alive
Those are the real moments
A proclivity to rise

I trust in myself implicitly
Face your demise
He pushed me too hard, I pushed back
Seeing with new eyes
A room full of mirrors
Can't find my way out
What was ripped away
I will always find an opening
I have nothing to hide
Something I was forced into
Let go of all the pain
A hate I restrain
A truth so strong, so deep
When there's no one there to help

Something to relieve the pressure
This existence so mysterious
A spirit so indefinite
Complications arise
Everything I specify
Constantly searching
When it seems so lucid

The filth I was drowning in
Getting closer to what I need
A gleam in the darkness caught my eye
Intense bravery
With these demons I collide
Work hard to get well

I will always optimize
Seeing results through time
A view so enthralling
Take it in, let it flow through you
A longing for peace
I won't sink so deep
Below the surface
I will eliminate this
Building an antivirus
Learning through osmosis
Breaking down walls
Give it time

Incentive pushing me, driving me
Deep wounds healing
Powerful feelings
Winning this battle
This fear is my enemy
I will conquer it

Always finding the right path
All you need is in you
Notions going through my mind

All the places I have been within
There was a moment of clarity
A surge of positive energy
When it's hard to break free from the binds
Life can be so intriguing
Also so difficult

Everything enveloping us
Reach for your higher being
Ripping, tearing beneath
A feeling deep within
It takes bravery
I was able to see into and through
So high I flew, to a new level
This persistence so ferocious
Being guided by something inside
At the bottom for so many years
There was a threatening darkness
There was a sickness

On the right course
What you can move with force

What lives inside us
What we have survived
My mind now more clear
An execution of honor
I will revel in the light
Sucked into the dark
Take it all in
Always carry it with you
Using this truth
A sinking inside
A feeling pulling me back
What we need to do to survive this
Trust in something more
The energy of life
Extraction of a deep infection
Finding ways to deal
A blessing in disguise
Save yourself from yourself
Help yourself
A struggling idealist
Went from nothing to something important
Against this reality
It's a miracle I'm alive

Moving with instinct
Negative effects

My motives are direct
When it's hard to accept
I will incapacitate this nemesis
Everything against me
The interconnections within, together functioning
I have travelled so far against the odds
It's not so far gone
I have all the answers I need
Humanity in distress
It's up to us to change

Appreciating life
Be proud of what you've done
It is what you make it
Something enclosed far within that I opened
It showed me there is more
What resides in the core
My nature is inherent
So many issues to deal with
What I use to fight with
I was stranded in another place
So far away
I was able to escape
Into new days
Negative feelings build up
Cleanse my spirit

Schizophrenia so irritating
I will stand against it
Gaining power and control

A hidden channel within
It can help you see
Everything that fell upon me
Everything I lifted up
I found my calling
An illness so pernicious
I was always falling

Completely regenerated
Dedicated to my cause
There was a strong impulse
Leading me through the danger
Control the anger
A visual transcendence
Everything I have found with my spirit
Born into darkness
If you look hard enough you can find light
I destroyed my past to build something new
I will face this abomination
A fatal wound that slowly heals
Lived through my atrocity
My ways are unique

No hypocrisy
Simplify, a logical approach
Let the sound hit you and take you places
My stasis keeping me together
Keeping my head right
Everything that keeps us alive
I have arrived at this destination
Restoration
There was an encumbrance
I had to break through
Those experiences that raise our hopes

A congruent form
Violent storms
Not so forlorn
Is it more than a test
Climbing mountains so high
Further and further
Embrace this freedom
Live free, die free
Feeling the spectrum of this existence
A puzzle of many parts
The brave will survive
In due time
Teach yourself to fly
Just getting by

Get up again
Gaining wisdom

Something infinite
Something beyond
I will make this better
Handling life for so long
There was a dense fog
Hard to see things clearly
Those times when I'm struggling to live
Went into the monster's lair
Came out alive
All the injustice I was put into

So grateful of where I have been
Everything I will defend
My repercussions, just part of the battle
Helps me push on
Survival instincts
The one that got away
The cold dark days
The life that opened up
The leech that sucks
The flame within lighting up the darkness
The steps you take to find yourself

My mind is strong
It took so long

The mistakes I have lived with
What I am doing is important
Take a moment to celebrate this life
An everlasting drive
Being conducive
Reaching out into the unknown
So high I have flown
Hope is not lost
Getting better all of the time, recovering
There is a disturbance
I will always pull through
I will not be dragged down by this unknown force
I will not be discouraged, I will lift myself up
The source of all of this was my relentless battle
Experience this life
My mind stares into this glare
Everything I take in
What I put out
This metamorphosis flowing through me
Put an end to the misery
We are here for a reason
I have made so much progress
When it gets intense

Everything I have I deserve
I had to work for it
My growth I observe
Found an antidote
A solution, an answer
The way you see yourself is what matters
How it looks through these eyes
How it all unfolds

What we are up against
I know I have what it takes
I can't explain it
Something trying to hold me down
My freedom no longer severed
To initiate logic
I will not let it take over
So much more to find
The old me died
A sickness that will not take control
Blocking out negativity
Never senseless
Something I have built within
There is good in this world
Even if it's so fucked up
Do not hold back
Give it everything you have

I know I will make it
Thrown into this world
When it's hard to take it
Build an equilibrium inside
Whatever keeps me on the right path
Fuck all the pettiness

It took a turn for the worst
A banishment of a curse
Something in me obscure
Not sure how it got in me
What we can reach
Myself I teach
We all have our battles, some worse
Learn how to get by
Never figured out why
Something taken by fear
I can't explain what I hear
Time and effort
What suddenly appears

A condition of great mental concentration
Or abstraction
All fucked up in a trance
It reached a point of wonder
What makes us whole

Pushing onward through the cold
Using my mind to win
I will clean my spirit
Apprehension grows, expands
What I give
Just want to live
Everything I refuse
Everything I use
What a human being will do to survive
The horror we go through
It's not the destination, it's the journey
A strong distinction

This thing inside me, diminished
There has been so much animosity, atrocity
Something eternal
I know it will always be there guiding me
I know what it's like to lose
What it takes to win
I know what I need to be
A staggering hope, lifeforce
Escaping devastation
This elation helping me see the good
The wars I have lived through
A reflection of light caught my eyes
Seeing further into something great

Something needed
An ominous, sinister cycle broken
Follow your heart into new lands of fortune
Embrace these emotions

I have suffered so much throughout the years
The torment slowly fades and disappears
Enjoyment arrives
I let it fill me
I let it take me away
An escape
A different state
This inquiry bringing me closer to what I am
looking for.

www.ingramcontent.com/pod-product-compliance
Lightning Source LLC
Chambersburg PA
CBHW021132020426
42331CB00005B/735